Little
Estuaries

Little Daniel Kramb
Estuaries

HETMOET

MENARD PRESS

Amsterdam * London

Where light swims,
slowly, to a some-
where:

Your
mind re-
thinks its territory

A shimmer –
vague but
likely:

This
distance is
no measure of belonging

Between the land
and the idea
of a land:

Each
surge,
division-less, a clearing

How mud, ex-
posed, re-
members:

The
slow sub-
side of scars

Not shore still.
Nor yet
sea:

Foot-
steps
of intent

In ever-shifting
sands, what
pattern:

No image
bolder than
these blanks

If, imagined,
a causeway
stretches:

Wash-
ed clean
corner of the mind

In nightfall's border
break, but
briefly:

What
only skin
can understand

When the construction
clears for you
to see:

Dawn
walk, bending.
The light beneath

Conceding ground,
at an edge,
afar:

The
inevitable
in waves of knowing

Bends silt-
ing as
hills:

You
cannot trust
yourself from here

Between the afar and
your cannot-bring-
near:

Raw
interiors,
hand-dishevelled

From alcoves, assumed,
low as
night:

Swept
skeletons
of a singing

Mud-sunken, you watch
your questions
salt:

And
tyrants
grow for answers

Winds, but for lower
weeds
alone:

One
clod
hardens

To energies,
aroused,
no line:

Each
breath,
infinity-inflected

Thought re-
turns as
shell:

Far
as these
flats allow

Mid-flat, where a feeling
ought
to be:

The
remem-
brance of stars

What's shaped
a stand-
point:

In quietly
dissolving,
no pebble hold

Between your looking
and its being
returned:

Stone-
turned longing
for the other side

Terrain-veiled walk,
assurance-
ward:

Dare
an afar to safety
with your looking

Waters,
seen a-
sunder:

Try build
your house
into the tidal flow

What yield from edge-
land's
scrap:

Rich
fractal
of a rising

Onset's lapping
inward-
led:

What's
loving in
your looking?

Where the images find
their projector-
current:

You
cannot
stand the sea from here

No birds a-
drift on
tidal:

These
streams
you make your own

Surfacing, one
into an-
other:

Sky's
line, in-
scribed as longing

Land-allied, your
threshold
fear:

Too
timid, waters'
taking you astray

Reds aglow as
evening's
extent:

Near-
by, a
feeling silts

The soil-ed and
heavy
stand:

Write
an ahead
with letting go

Clouds cracked. A low
light shim-
mer:

Strength
like a gust
in your bones

Salt, un-sluiced,
in inland
flow:

From
banks
benumbed, no answer

Sepia-turned,
stones of
a chapel:

One
stream and
another, merging

Water-borne,
a surface
calm:

Held,
half-sub-
merged, a-mend

Where seeing
carves its
cavity:

Trace
of a bolden-
ing response

Erased from a grey-
graded
sky:

No
gleam
but from below

Exposed, as naked,
in re-
treat:

A
slow
approaching, in attempts

Attachment dries
a trickle
dream:

No
signage
to a seabed trail

Mind-folded,
your outer
stretch:

Eyes
catch
a certainty for you

Yielding definition
to each side's
shore:

But
hills are still
conceivable, here

Swept together on a bright
white
light:

Re-
luctant-
ly, life's ebbing

Your figure, shadowless
as
X:

No
tremor
beneath faith-clad hands

Towards the
sky you
sculpt:

Tide-
taken.
Its cannot-swim

Unobserved, night's
nearing and
retreat:

Leaving
the pebbles re-
arranged. No pattern

In the persistence
of a
ray:

A
surge, fore-
seen, is diminished

Feet as if
on finer
ground:

Where's
endurance
in this stretch

Washed, towards
bare feet, as
words:

There is
no keeping,
here. No translation

Where turning does
not change per-
spective:

Steps
getting
lighter with each step

To divine, standing
border-less,
no land:

The
body
responds, off-mind

Suspended, sphere
edge, listen-
ing:

More
light than
you can muster

Enclosed by
safety's
lock:

But
from within,
the borders redraw

Wrapped,
as if by
bodies:

A
tide
that leaves with nothing

ACKNOWLEDGEMENTS

Thanks to *The London Magazine* and *Prototype*, where
some of these poems first appeared. To Lucy Binnersley, for
opening collaboration's door and connecting me to Louisa.
Thank you, Louisa Albani, for the purest of collaborations,
and your magical cover art. For your ongoing belief in my
work, Jess Chandler, thank you.
To Rishi Dastidar, for reading an early draft – vital in shaping
these pieces. Thanks to everyone at Metal Southend, for all
your support, and the SEE Park commission in particular.
To Elte Rauch and everyone at HetMoet-Menard, for
receiving the *Estuaries* in such a beautiful way and giving
them their dream home on the page – thank you. For always
being by my side, Nico (you little poet). To Jean – for the
love that feeds everything.

ABOUT THE AUTHOR

Daniel Kramb is a writer and poet. He is a member of Malika's Poetry Kitchen and his prose history of the collective is out in *Too Young, Too Loud, Too Different* (2021). Other work has appeared in *The London Magazine*, *Prototype*, *Popshot* and elsewhere. His fiction includes *Central* (2015) and *From Here* (2012). Several *Little Estuaries* make up a poetry intervention at Thameside Nature Reserve commissioned for South Essex Estuary (SEE) Park by URBAN landscape architects and arts organisation Metal Southend (metalculture.com).

ABOUT THE PUBLISHERS

HetMoet-Menard Press is the London based imprint of HetMoet Publishing; an indie press based on a historic sailing barge in Amsterdam, the Netherlands and was founded by Elte Rauch in 2018. The Menard Press was founded by Anthony Rudolf in 1979.

Please get in touch at menard@hetmoet.com
or write to 8 The Oaks, Woodside Avenue, London N12 8AR

Visit www.hetmoet-menardpress.co.uk
Follow us on
 @Hetmoet_Menard
@menardpress_hetmoet

This edition was first published in The United Kingdom in 2023
by HetMoet-Menard Press

Copyright © Daniel Kramb, 2023
Cover artwork © Louisa Albani, 2022

Daniel Kramb asserts the moral right to be identified as the author of this
work in accordance with the Copyright, Designs and Patents Act 1988
A CIP catalogue record for this book is available from the British Library

ISBN 9789083312613

Editing by Elte Rauch & Ilse van Oosten
Typeset in IvyPresto Text by Ivy Foundry
Book design by Armée de Verre Bookdesign, Ghent, Belgium
Printed and bound in Belgium by Graphius
Distributed by InPress Ltd Newcastle upon Thyme

www.hetmoet-menardpress.co.uk